50 Great Poems to Read & Perform Out Loud

For Students, Actors and Lovers of Reading Poetry

Edited by Carl Scott Harker

TABLE OF CONTENTS

Dedication .... Page 5

Introduction .... Page 6

The Poems

Dedication

Around 1978, I had the good fortune to become a volunteer reader at the Radio for the Blind in San Francisco. At that time, the Radio for the Blind was a special broadcast system that used a radio frequency that was exclusively used for radio receivers provided to those who were blind. This was before the digital age and streaming audio. And pretty much before the books on tape market boomed. Today, such services for the blind have morphed into streaming content online, podcasts and audible books.

Anyway, at that time, volunteers at the Radio for the Blind station would read daily newspapers like the San Francisco Chronicle and magazines as well as spend time in small studios recording books for scheduled broadcasts. And I got to read poetry.

I, with a co-recorder, created thirty-three 1/2-hour poetry readings, where the two of us read all kinds of poetry. Western ballads, the Romantics, and a great variety of poems from Homer to Ferlinghetti. The series enjoyed some success, as it was syndicated for use in other cities.

For more than thirty-five weeks, all we thought about was poetry – researching and finding poems in the library and in old books. Reading them over and over and finding those bits of poetry that would fit together thematically and time wise. It is from that experience, as well as other chances to read poetry out loud, that I have drawn the poems you will find in this book.

And in remembrance of that period of immersion in all words poetry, I wish to dedicate this book to that partner in rhyme, Ellen Holzman.

Introduction

In this book, you will find some of the greatest poetry ever written. Even more, this book contains work that becomes even better when read out loud. Every syllable become likes notes in a symphony, creating chords along with the definition of the words they assemble.

You can enjoy these poems silently in your mind. But they should be read aloud, so that the sounds you create as you read are allowed to add another level of meaning to the words spoken.

As the words flow through your vocal cords, do not be surprised to find a force coursing through you as well. It is the force of poetry – words distilled down to their essences - transporting you to new vistas, new understanding and new experiences.

I believe this book will be useful to students, actors, the shy, and those who speak English as a second language. Those who read these poems will discover a richer language and deeper understandings. Let each word in these poems twist your tongues into the sound shapes they demand and discover the power of the spoken word.

After the end of the section containing the poems within this book, you will find some brief notes or my comments about the individual poems for your enjoyment and elucidation.

~ Carl Scott Harker

"Ozymandias" by Percy Bysshe Shelley (1792-1822)

I met a traveler from an antique land
Who said: "Two vast and trunkless legs of stone
Stand in the desert . . . Near them, on the sand,
Half sunk, a shattered visage lies, whose frown,
And wrinkled lip, and sneer of cold command,
Tell that its sculptor well those passions read
Which yet survive, stamped on these lifeless things,
The hand that mocked them, and the heart that fed:
And on the pedestal these words appear:
'My name is Ozymandias, king of kings:
Look on my works, ye Mighty, and despair!'
Nothing beside remains. Round the decay
Of that colossal wreck, boundless and bare
The lone and level sands stretch far away."

"You are old, Father William" (1865) by Lewis Carroll

"You are old, Father William," the young man said,
"And your hair has become very white;
And yet you incessantly stand on your head –
Do you think, at your age, it is right?"

"In my youth," Father William replied to his son,
"I feared it might injure the brain;
But, now that I'm perfectly sure I have none,
Why, I do it again and again."

"You are old," said the youth, "as I mentioned before,
And have grown most uncommonly fat;
Yet you turned a back-somersault in at the door –
Pray, what is the reason of that?"

"In my youth," said the sage, as he shook his grey locks,
"I kept all my limbs very supple
By the use of this ointment – one shilling the box –
Allow me to sell you a couple?"

"You are old," said the youth, "and your jaws are too weak
For anything tougher than suet;
Yet you finished the goose, with the bones and the beak –
Pray, how did you manage to do it?"

"In my youth," said his father, "I took to the law,
And argued each case with my wife;
And the muscular strength, which it gave to my jaw,
Has lasted the rest of my life."

"You are old," said the youth, "one would hardly suppose
That your eye was as steady as ever;
Yet you balanced an eel on the end of your nose –
What made you so awfully clever?"

"I have answered three questions, and that is enough,"
Said his father; "don't give yourself airs!
Do you think I can listen all day to such stuff?
Be off, or I'll kick you downstairs!"

"The Owl and the Pussycat" by Edward Lear

The Owl and the Pussy Cat went to sea
In a beautiful pea-green boat,
They took some honey, and plenty of money
Wrapped up in a five-pound note.
The Owl looked up to the stars above,
And sang to a small guitar,
"O lovely Pussy, O Pussy, my love,
What a beautiful Pussy you are,
You are,
You are!
What a beautiful Pussy you are!"

Pussy said to the Owl, "You elegant fowl!
How charmingly sweet you sing!
O let us be married! too long we have tarried:
But what shall we do for a ring?"
They sailed away, for a year and a day,
To the land where the Bong-tree grows
And there in a wood a Piggy-wig stood
With a ring at the end of his nose,
His nose,
His nose,
With a ring at the end of his nose.

"Dear Pig, are you willing to sell for one shilling
Your ring?" Said the Piggy, "I will."
So they took it away, and were married next day
By the Turkey who lives on the hill.
They dined on mince, and slices of quince,
Which they ate with a runcible spoon;
And hand in hand, on the edge of the sand,
They danced by the light of the moon,
The moon,
The moon,
They danced by the light of the moon.

"No Man is an Island" by John Donne

No man is an island,
Entire of itself,
Every man is a piece of the continent,
A part of the main.
If a clod be washed away by the sea,
Europe is the less.
As well as if a promontory were.
As well as if a manor of thy friend's
Or of thine own were:
Any man's death diminishes me,
Because I am involved in mankind,
And therefore never send to know for whom the bell tolls;
It tolls for thee.

"The Charge of the Light Brigade" by Alfred, Lord Tennyson

I

Half a league, half a league,
Half a league onward,
All in the valley of Death
Rode the six hundred.
"Forward, the Light Brigade!
Charge for the guns!" he said.
Into the valley of Death
Rode the six hundred.

II

"Forward, the Light Brigade!"
Was there a man dismayed?
Not though the soldier knew
Someone had blundered.
Theirs not to make reply,
Theirs not to reason why,
Theirs but to do and die.
Into the valley of Death
Rode the six hundred.

III

Cannon to right of them,
Cannon to left of them,
Cannon in front of them
Volleyed and thundered;
Stormed at with shot and shell,
Boldly they rode and well,
Into the jaws of Death,
Into the mouth of hell
Rode the six hundred.

IV

Flashed all their sabres bare,
Flashed as they turned in air
Sabring the gunners there,
Charging an army, while
All the world wondered.
Plunged in the battery-smoke
Right through the line they broke;
Cossack and Russian
Reeled from the sabre stroke
Shattered and sundered.
Then they rode back, but not
Not the six hundred.

V

Cannon to right of them,
Cannon to left of them,
Cannon behind them
Volleyed and thundered;
Stormed at with shot and shell,
While horse and hero fell.
They that had fought so well
Came through the jaws of Death,
Back from the mouth of hell,
All that was left of them,
Left of six hundred.

VI

When can their glory fade?
O the wild charge they made!
All the world wondered.
Honour the charge they made!
Honour the Light Brigade,
Noble six hundred!

"Kubla Khan" by Samuel Taylor Coleridge
Or, a vision in a dream. A Fragment.

In Xanadu did Kubla Khan
A stately pleasure-dome decree:
Where Alph, the sacred river, ran
Through caverns measureless to man
   Down to a sunless sea.
So twice five miles of fertile ground
With walls and towers were girdled round;
And there were gardens bright with sinuous rills,
Where blossomed many an incense-bearing tree;
And here were forests ancient as the hills,
Enfolding sunny spots of greenery.

But oh! that deep romantic chasm which slanted
Down the green hill athwart a cedarn cover!
A savage place! as holy and enchanted
As e'er beneath a waning moon was haunted
By woman wailing for her demon-lover!
And from this chasm, with ceaseless turmoil seething,
As if this earth in fast thick pants were breathing,
A mighty fountain momently was forced:
Amid whose swift half-intermitted burst
Huge fragments vaulted like rebounding hail,
Or chaffy grain beneath the thresher's flail:
And mid these dancing rocks at once and ever
It flung up momently the sacred river.
Five miles meandering with a mazy motion
Through wood and dale the sacred river ran,
Then reached the caverns measureless to man,
And sank in tumult to a lifeless ocean;
And 'mid this tumult Kubla heard from far
Ancestral voices prophesying war!
   The shadow of the dome of pleasure
   Floated midway on the waves;
   Where was heard the mingled measure
   From the fountain and the caves.
It was a miracle of rare device,
A sunny pleasure-dome with caves of ice!

(continued next page)

A damsel with a dulcimer
In a vision once I saw:
It was an Abyssinian maid
And on her dulcimer she played,
Singing of Mount Abora.
Could I revive within me
Her symphony and song,
To such a deep delight 'twould win me,
That with music loud and long,
I would build that dome in air,
That sunny dome! those caves of ice!
And all who heard should see them there,
And all should cry, Beware! Beware!
His flashing eyes, his floating hair!
Weave a circle round him thrice,
And close your eyes with holy dread
For he on honey-dew hath fed,
And drunk the milk of Paradise.

"Ulysses" by Alfred Lord Tennyson

It little profits that an idle king,
By this still hearth, among these barren crags,
Match'd with an aged wife, I mete and dole
Unequal laws unto a savage race,
That hoard, and sleep, and feed, and know not me.
I cannot rest from travel: I will drink
Life to the lees: All times I have enjoy'd
Greatly, have suffer'd greatly, both with those
That loved me, and alone, on shore, and when
Thro' scudding drifts the rainy Hyades
Vext the dim sea: I am become a name;
For always roaming with a hungry heart
Much have I seen and known; cities of men
And manners, climates, councils, governments,
Myself not least, but honour'd of them all;
And drunk delight of battle with my peers,
Far on the ringing plains of windy Troy.
I am a part of all that I have met;
Yet all experience is an arch wherethro'
Gleams that untravell'd world whose margin fades
For ever and forever when I move.
How dull it is to pause, to make an end,
To rust unburnish'd, not to shine in use!
As tho' to breathe were life! Life piled on life
Were all too little, and of one to me
Little remains: but every hour is saved
From that eternal silence, something more,
A bringer of new things; and vile it were
For some three suns to store and hoard myself,
And this gray spirit yearning in desire
To follow knowledge like a sinking star,
Beyond the utmost bound of human thought.

This is my son, mine own Telemachus,
To whom I leave the sceptre and the isle,—
Well-loved of me, discerning to fulfil
This labour, by slow prudence to make mild

(continued next page)

A rugged people, and thro' soft degrees
Subdue them to the useful and the good.
Most blameless is he, centred in the sphere
Of common duties, decent not to fail
In offices of tenderness, and pay
Meet adoration to my household gods,
When I am gone. He works his work, I mine.

There lies the port; the vessel puffs her sail:
There gloom the dark, broad seas. My mariners,
Souls that have toil'd, and wrought, and thought with me—
That ever with a frolic welcome took
The thunder and the sunshine, and opposed
Free hearts, free foreheads—you and I are old;
Old age hath yet his honour and his toil;
Death closes all: but something ere the end,
Some work of noble note, may yet be done,
Not unbecoming men that strove with Gods.
The lights begin to twinkle from the rocks:
The long day wanes: the slow moon climbs: the deep
Moans round with many voices. Come, my friends,
'T is not too late to seek a newer world.
Push off, and sitting well in order smite
The sounding furrows; for my purpose holds
To sail beyond the sunset, and the baths
Of all the western stars, until I die.
It may be that the gulfs will wash us down:
It may be we shall touch the Happy Isles,
And see the great Achilles, whom we knew.
Tho' much is taken, much abides; and tho'
We are not now that strength which in old days
Moved earth and heaven, that which we are, we are;
One equal temper of heroic hearts,
Made weak by time and fate, but strong in will
To strive, to seek, to find, and not to yield.

"In Flanders Fields" by John McCrae

In Flanders fields the poppies blow
Between the crosses, row on row,
That mark our place: and in the sky
The larks still bravely singing fly
Scarce heard amid the guns below.

We are the dead: Short days ago,
We lived, felt dawn, saw sunset glow,
Loved and were loved: and now we lie
In Flanders fields!

Take up our quarrel with the foe
To you, from failing hands, we throw
The torch: be yours to hold it high
If ye break faith with us who die,
We shall not sleep, though poppies grow
In Flanders fields.

"Columbus" by Joaquin Miller (1892)

Behind him lay the gray Azores,
Behind the Gates of Hercules;
Before him not the ghost of shores,
Before him only shoreless seas.
The good mate said: "Now must we pray,
For lo! the very stars are gone.
Brave Admiral, speak, what shall I say?"
"Why, say, 'Sail on! sail on! and on!'"

"My men grow mutinous day by day;
My men grow ghastly wan and weak."
The stout mate thought of home; a spray
Of salt wave washed his swarthy cheek.
"What shall I say, brave Admiral, say,
If we sight naught but seas at dawn?"
"Why, you shall say at break of day,
'Sail on! sail on! sail on! and on!'"

They sailed and sailed, as winds might blow,
Until at last the blanched mate said:
"Why, now not even God would know
Should I and all my men fall dead.
These very winds forget their way,
For God from these dread seas is gone.
Now speak, brave Admiral, speak and say"—
He said: "Sail on! sail on! and on!"

They sailed. They sailed. Then spake the mate:
"This mad sea shows his teeth to-night.
He curls his lip, he lies in wait,
With lifted teeth, as if to bite!
Brave Admiral, say but one good word:
What shall we do when hope is gone?"
The words leapt like a leaping sword:
"Sail on! sail on! sail on! and on!"

(continued next page)

Then, pale and worn, he kept his deck,
And peered through darkness. Ah, that night
Of all dark nights! And then a speck—

A light! A light! A light! A light!
It grew, a starlit flag unfurled!
It grew to be Time's burst of dawn.
He gained a world; he gave that world
Its grandest lesson: "On! sail on!"

"Jabberwocky" by Lewis Carroll

'Twas brillig, and the slithy toves
    Did gyre and gimble in the wabe;
All mimsy were the borogoves,
    And the mome raths outgrabe.

"Beware the Jabberwock, my son
    The jaws that bite, the claws that catch!
Beware the Jubjub bird, and shun
    The frumious Bandersnatch!"

He took his vorpal sword in hand;
    Long time the manxome foe he sought—
So rested he by the Tumtum tree,
    And stood awhile in thought.

And, as in uffish thought he stood,
    The Jabberwock, with eyes of flame,
Came whiffling through the tulgey wood,
    And burbled as it came!

One, two! One, two! And through and through
    The vorpal blade went snicker-snack!
He left it dead, and with its head
    He went galumphing back.

"And hast thou slain the Jabberwock?
    Come to my arms, my beamish boy!
O frabjous day! Callooh! Callay!"
    He chortled in his joy.

'Twas brillig, and the slithy toves
    Did gyre and gimble in the wabe;
All mimsy were the borogoves,
    And the mome raths outgrabe.

"Some One" by Walter de la Mare

Some one came knocking
At my wee, small door;
Someone came knocking;
I'm sure-sure-sure;
I listened, I opened,
I looked to left and right,
But nought there was a stirring
In the still dark night;
Only the busy beetle
Tap-tapping in the wall,
Only from the forest
The screech-owl's call,
Only the cricket whistling
While the dewdrops fall,
So I know not who came knocking,
At all, at all, at all.

"Witches Spell Poem" by William Shakespeare

Thrice the brinded cat hath mew'd.
Thrice and once the hedge-pig whined.

Harpier cries 'Tis time, 'tis time.
Round about the cauldron go;
In the poison'd entrails throw.
Toad, that under cold stone
Days and nights has thirty-one
Swelter'd venom sleeping got,
Boil thou first i' the charmed pot.

Double, double toil and trouble;
Fire burn, and cauldron bubble.

Fillet of a fenny snake,
In the cauldron boil and bake;
Eye of newt and toe of frog,
Wool of bat and tongue of dog,
Adder's fork and blind-worm's sting,
Lizard's leg and owlet's wing,
For a charm of powerful trouble,
Like a hell-broth boil and bubble.

Double, double toil and trouble;
Fire burn and cauldron bubble.

Scale of dragon, tooth of wolf,
Witches' mummy, maw and gulf
Of the ravin'd salt-sea shark,
Root of hemlock digg'd i' the dark,
Liver of blaspheming Jew,
Gall of goat, and slips of yew
Sliver'd in the moon's eclipse,
Nose of Turk and Tartar's lips,
Finger of birth-strangled babe
Ditch-deliver'd by a drab,
Make the gruel thick and slab:
Add thereto a tiger's chaudron,
For the ingredients of our cauldron.

Double, double toil and trouble;
Fire burn and cauldron bubble.

Cool it with a baboon's blood,
Then the charm is firm and good.

"On The Landing" by Francis Bret Harte

(AN IDYL OF THE BALUSTERS)

Editor's note: This poem is read as if it was a scene from a play with two characters: BOBBY, age 3 ½, JOHNNY, age 4 1/2.

BOBBY

Do you know why they've put us in that back room,
Up in the attic, close against the sky,
And made believe our nursery's a cloak-room?
Do you know why?

JOHNNY

No more I don't, nor why that Sammy's mother,
What Ma thinks horrid, 'cause he bunged my eye,
Eats an ice cream, down there, like any other!
No more don't I!

BOBBY

Do you know why Nurse says it isn't manners
For you and me to ask folks twice for pie,
And no one hits that man with two bananas?
Do you know why?

JOHNNY

No more I don't, nor why that girl, whose dress is
Off of her shoulders, don't catch cold and die,
When you and me gets croup when WE undresses!
No more don't I!

(continued next page)

BOBBY

Perhaps she ain't as good as you and I is,
And God don't want her up there in the sky,
And lets her live--to come in just when pie is--
Perhaps that's why!

JOHNNY

Do you know why that man that's got a cropped head
Rubbed it just now as if he felt a fly?
Could it be, Bobby, something that I dropded?
And is that why?

BOBBY

Good boys behaves, and so they don't get scolded,
Nor drop hot milk on folks as they pass by.

JOHNNY (piously)

Marbles would bounce on Mr. Jones' bald head--
But I sha'n't try!

BOBBY

Do you know why Aunt Jane is always snarling
At you and me because we tells a lie,
And she don't slap that man that called her darling?
Do you know why?

JOHNNY

No more I don't, nor why that man with Mamma
Just kissed her hand.

(continued next page)

BOBBY

She hurt it--and that's why;
He made it well, the very way that Mamma
Does do to I.

JOHNNY

I feel so sleepy. . . . Was that Papa kissed us?
What made him sigh, and look up to the sky?

BOBBY

We weren't downstairs, and he and God had missed us,
And that was why!

"A Red, Red Rose" by Robert Burns

O my Luve is like a red, red rose
    That's newly sprung in June;
O my Luve is like the melody
    That's sweetly played in tune.

So fair art thou, my bonnie lass,
    So deep in luve am I;
And I will luve thee still, my dear,
    Till a' the seas gang dry.

Till a' the seas gang dry, my dear,
    And the rocks melt wi' the sun;
I will love thee still, my dear,
    While the sands o' life shall run.

And fare thee weel, my only luve!
    And fare thee weel awhile!
And I will come again, my luve,
    Though it were ten thousand mile.

"The Ballad of How MacPherson Held the Floor" by Robert Service

Said President MacConnachie to Treasurer MacCall:
"We ought to have a piper for our next Saint Andrew's Ball.
Yon squakin' saxophone gives me the syncopated gripes.
I'm sick of jazz, I want to hear the skirling of the pipes."
"Alas! it's true," said Tam MacCall. "The young folk of to-day
Are fox-trot mad and dinna ken a reel from Strathspey.
Now, what we want's a kiltie lad, primed up wi' mountain dew,
To strut the floor at supper time, and play a lilt or two.
In all the North there's only one; of him I've heard them speak:
His name is Jock MacPherson, and he lives on Boulder Creek;
An old-time hard-rock miner, and a wild and wastrel loon,
Who spends his nights in glory, playing pibrochs to the moon.
I'll seek him out; beyond a doubt on next Saint Andrew's night
We'll proudly hear the pipes to cheer and charm our appetite.

Oh lads were neat and lassies sweet who graced Saint Andrew's Ball;
But there was none so full of fun as Treasurer MacCall.
And as Maloney's rag-time bank struck up the newest hit,
He smiled a smile behind his hand, and chuckled: "Wait a bit."
And so with many a Celtic snort, with malice in his eye,
He watched the merry crowd cavort, till supper time drew nigh.
Then gleefully he seemed to steal, and sought the Nugget Bar,
Wherein there sat a tartaned chiel, as lonely as a star;
A huge and hairy Highlandman as hearty as a breeze,
A glass of whisky in his hand, his bag-pipes on his knees.
"Drink down your doch and doris, Jock," cried Treasurer MacCall;
"The time is ripe to up and pipe; they wait you in the hall.
Gird up your loins and grit your teeth, and here's a pint of hooch
To mind you of your native heath - jist pit it in your pooch.
Play on and on for all you're worth; you'll shame us if you stop.
Remember you're of Scottish birth - keep piping till you drop.
Aye, though a bunch of Willie boys should bluster and implore,
For the glory of the Highlands, lad, you've got to hold the floor."
The dancers were at supper, and the tables groaned with cheer,
When President MacConnachie exclaimed: "What do I hear?
Methinks it's like a chanter, and its coming from the hall."   (continued next page)

"It's Jock MacPherson tuning up," cried Treasurer MacCall.
So up they jumped with shouts of glee, and gaily hurried forth.
Said they: "We never thought to see a piper in the North."
Aye, all the lads and lassies braw went buzzing out like bees,
And Jock MacPherson there they saw, with red and rugged knees.
Full six foot four he strode the floor, a grizzled son of Skye,
With glory in his whiskers and with whisky in his eye.
With skelping stride and Scottish pride he towered above them all:
"And is he no' a bonny sight?" said Treasurer MacCall.
While President MacConnachie was fairly daft with glee,
And there was jubilation in the Scottish Commy-tee.
But the dancers seemed uncertain, and they signified their doubt,
By dashing back to eat as fast as they had darted out.
And someone raised the question 'twixt the coffee and the cakes:
"Does the Piper walk to get away from all the noise he makes?"
Then reinforced with fancy food they slowly trickled forth,
And watching in patronizing mood the Piper of the North.

Proud, proud was Jock MacPherson, as he made his bag-pipes skirl,
And he set his sporran swinging, and he gave his kilts a whirl.
And President MacConnachie was jumping like a flea,
And there was joy and rapture in the Scottish Commy-tee.
"Jist let them have their saxophones wi' constipated squall;
We're having Heaven's music now," said Treasurer MacCall.
But the dancers waxed impatient, and they rather seemed to fret
For Maloney and the jazz of his Hibernian Quartette.
Yet little recked the Piper, as he swung with head on high,
Lamenting with MacCrimmon on the heather hills of Skye.
With Highland passion in his heart he held the centre floor;
Aye, Jock MacPherson played as he had never played before.

Maloney's Irish melodists were sitting in their place,
And as Maloney waited, there was wonder in his face.
'Twas sure the gorgeous music - Golly! wouldn't it be grand
If he could get MacPherson as a member of his band?
But the dancers moped and mumbled, as around the room they sat:
"We paid to dance," they grumbled; "But we cannot dance to that.
Of course we're not denying that it's really splendid stuff;
But it's mighty satisfying - don't you think we've had enough?" (continued next page)

"You've raised a pretty problem," answered Treasurer MacCall;
"For on Saint Andrew's Night, ye ken, the Piper rules the Ball."
Said President MacConnachie: "You've said a solemn thing.
Tradition holds him sacred, and he's got to have his fling.
But soon, no doubt, he'll weary out. Have patience; bide a wee."
"That's right. Respect the Piper," said the Scottish Commy-tee.

And so MacPherson stalked the floor, and fast the moments flew,
Till half an hour went past, as irritation grew and grew.
Then the dancers held a council, and with faces fiercely set,
They hailed Maloney, heading his Hibernian Quartette:
"It's long enough, we've waited. Come on, Mike, play up the Blues."
And Maloney hesitated, but he didn't dare refuse.
So banjo and piano, and guitar and saxophone
Contended with the shrilling of the chanter and the drone;
And the women's ears were muffled, so infernal was the din,
But MacPherson was unruffled, for he knew that he would win.
Then two bright boys jazzed round him, and they sought to play the clown,
But MacPherson jolted sideways, and the Sassenachs went down.
And as if it was a signal, with a wild and angry roar,
The gates of wrath were riven - yet MacPherson held the floor.

Aye, amid the rising tumult, still he strode with head on high,
With ribbands gaily streaming, yet with battle in his eye.
Amid the storm that gathered, still he stalked with Highland pride,
While President and Treasurer sprang bravely to his side.
And with ire and indignation that was glorious to see,
Around him in a body ringed the Scottish Commy-tee.
Their teeth were clenched with fury; their eyes with anger blazed:
"Ye manna touch the Piper," was the slogan that they raised.
Then blows were struck, and men went down; yet 'mid the rising fray
MacPherson towered in triumph – and he never ceased to play.

Alas! his faithful followers were but a gallant few,
And faced defeat, although they fought with all the skill they knew.
For President MacConnachie was seen to slip and fall,
And o'er his prostrate body stumbled Treasurer MacCall.
And as their foes with triumph roared, and leagured them about,
It looked as if their little band would soon be counted out.
For eyes were black and noses red, yet on that field of gore,   (continued next page)

As resolute as Highland rock - MacPherson held the floor.
Maloney watched the battle, and his brows were bleakly set,
While with him paused and panted his Hibernian Quartette.
For sure it is an evil spite, and breaking to the heart,
For Irishman to watch a fight and not be taking part.
Then suddenly on high he soared, and tightened up his belt:
"And shall we see them crush," he roared, "a brother and a Celt?
A fellow artiste needs our aid. Come on, boys, take a hand."
Then down into the mêlée dashed Maloney and his band.

Now though it was Saint Andrew's Ball, yet men of every race,
That bow before the Great God Jazz were gathered in that place.
Yea, there were those who grunt: "Ya! Ya!" and those who squeak: "We! We!"
Likewise Dutch, Dago, Swede and Finn, Polack and Portugee.
Yet like ripe grain before the gale that national hotch-potch
Went down before the fury of the Irish and the Scotch.
Aye, though they closed their gaping ranks and rallied to the fray,
To the Shamrock and the Thistle went the glory of the day.

You should have seen the carnage in the drooling light of dawn,
Yet 'mid the scene of slaughter Jock MacPherson playing on.
Though all lay low about him, yet he held his head on high,
And piped as if he stood upon the caller crags of Skye.
His face was grim as granite, and no favour did he ask,
Though weary were his mighty lungs and empty was his flask.
And when a fallen foe wailed out: "Say! when will you have done?"
MacPherson grinned and answered: "Hoots! She's only ha'f begun."
Aye, though his hands were bloody, and his knees were gay with gore,
A Grampian of Highland pride - MacPherson held the floor.

And still in Yukon valleys where the silent peaks look down,
They tell of how the Piper was invited up to town,
And he went in kilted glory, and he piped before them all,
But wouldn't stop his piping till he busted up the Ball.
Of that Homeric scrap they speak, and how the fight went on,
With sally and with rally till the breaking of the dawn.
And how the Piper towered like a rock amid the fray,
And the battle surged about him, but he never ceased to play.
Aye, by the lonely camp-fires, still they tell the story o'er-
How the Sassenach was vanquished and - MacPherson held the floor.

"I heard a Fly buzz - when I died" - (591) by Emily Dickinson

I heard a Fly buzz - when I died -
The Stillness in the Room
Was like the Stillness in the Air -
Between the Heaves of Storm -

The Eyes around - had wrung them dry -
And Breaths were gathering firm
For that last Onset - when the King
Be witnessed - in the Room -

I willed my Keepsakes - Signed away
What portion of me be
Assignable - and then it was
There interposed a Fly -

With Blue - uncertain - stumbling Buzz -
Between the light - and me -
And then the Windows failed - and then
I could not see to see -

"Rubáiyát of Omar Khayyám" translated by Edward FitzGerald
(three selected quatrains)

LXXI
The Moving Finger writes; and, having writ,
Moves on: nor all your Piety nor Wit
Shall lure it back to cancel half a Line,
Nor all your Tears wash out a Word of it.

XII
A Book of Verses underneath the Bough,
A Jug of Wine, a Loaf of Bread--and Thou
Beside me singing in the Wilderness--
Oh, Wilderness were Paradise enow!

XLVI (First Edition)
For in and out, above, about, below,
'Tis nothing but a Magic Shadow-show,
    Play'd in a Box whose Candle is the Sun,
Round which we Phantom Figures come and go.

"To the Virgins, to Make Much of Time" by Robert Herrick

Gather ye rosebuds while ye may,
  Old Time is still a-flying;
And this same flower that smiles today
  Tomorrow will be dying.

The glorious lamp of heaven, the sun,
  The higher he's a-getting,
The sooner will his race be run,
  And nearer he's to setting.

That age is best which is the first,
  When youth and blood are warmer;
But being spent, the worse, and worst
  Times still succeed the former.

Then be not coy, but use your time,
  And while ye may, go marry;
For having lost but once your prime,
  You may forever tarry.

"Death and Life" by Robert William Service

'Twas in the grave-yard's gruesome gloom
That May and I were mated;
We sneaked inside and on a tomb
Our love was consummated.
It's quite all right, no doubt we'll wed,
Our sin will go unchidden . . .
Ah! sweeter than the nuptial bed
Are ecstasies forbidden.

And as I held my sweetheart close,
And she was softly sighing,
I could not help but think of those
In peace below us lying.
Poor folks! No disrespect we meant,
And beg you'll be forgiving;
We hopes the dead will not resent
The rapture of the living.

And when in death I, too, shall lie,
And lost to those who love me,
I wish two sweethearts roving by
Will plight their troth above me.
Oh do not think that I will grieve
To hear the vows they're voicing,
And if their love new life conceive,
'Tis I will be rejoicing.

"Annabel Lee" by Edgar Allan Poe

It was many and many a year ago,
   In a kingdom by the sea,
That a maiden there lived whom you may know
   By the name of Annabel Lee;
And this maiden she lived with no other thought
   Than to love and be loved by me.

I was a child and *she* was a child,
   In this kingdom by the sea,
But we loved with a love that was more than love—
   I and my Annabel Lee—
With a love that the wingèd seraphs of Heaven
   Coveted her and me.

And this was the reason that, long ago,
   In this kingdom by the sea,
A wind blew out of a cloud, chilling
   My beautiful Annabel Lee;
So that her highborn kinsmen came
   And bore her away from me,
To shut her up in a sepulchre
   In this kingdom by the sea.

The angels, not half so happy in Heaven,
   Went envying her and me—
Yes!—that was the reason (as all men know,
   In this kingdom by the sea)
That the wind came out of the cloud by night,
   Chilling and killing my Annabel Lee.

But our love it was stronger by far than the love
   Of those who were older than we—
   Of many far wiser than we—
And neither the angels in Heaven above
   Nor the demons down under the sea
Can ever dissever my soul from the soul
   Of the beautiful Annabel Lee;

(continued next page)

For the moon never beams, without bringing me dreams
   Of the beautiful Annabel Lee;
And the stars never rise, but I feel the bright eyes
   Of the beautiful Annabel Lee;
And so, all the night-tide, I lie down by the side
   Of my darling—my darling—my life and my bride,
   In her sepulchre there by the sea—
   In her tomb by the sounding sea.

"Sudden Light" by Dante Gabriel Rossetti

I have been here before,
But when or how I cannot tell:
I know the grass beyond the door,
The sweet keen smell,
The sighing sound, the lights around the shore.

You have been mine before,—
How long ago I may not know:
But just when at that swallow's soar
Your neck turn'd so,
Some veil did fall,—I knew it all of yore.

Has this been thus before?
And shall not thus time's eddying flight
Still with our lives our love restore
In death's despite,
And day and night yield one delight once more?

"Pippa's Song" by Robert Browning

THE year's at the spring,
And day's at the morn;
Morning's at seven;
The hill-side's dew-pearl'd;
The lark's on the wing;
The snail's on the thorn;
God's in His heaven—
All's right with the world!

"The Raven" by Edgar Allan Poe

Once upon a midnight dreary, while I pondered, weak and weary,
Over many a quaint and curious volume of forgotten lore—
While I nodded, nearly napping, suddenly there came a tapping,
As of some one gently rapping, rapping at my chamber door—
"'Tis some visitor," I muttered, "tapping at my chamber door—
  Only this and nothing more."

Ah, distinctly I remember it was in the bleak December;
And each separate dying ember wrought its ghost upon the floor.
Eagerly I wished the morrow;—vainly I had sought to borrow
From my books surcease of sorrow—sorrow for the lost Lenore—
For the rare and radiant maiden whom the angels name Lenore—
  Nameless *here* for evermore.

And the silken, sad, uncertain rustling of each purple curtain
Thrilled me—filled me with fantastic terrors never felt before;
So that now, to still the beating of my heart, I stood repeating,
"'Tis some visitor entreating entrance at my chamber door—
Some late visitor entreating entrance at my chamber door;—
  This it is and nothing more."

Presently my soul grew stronger; hesitating then no longer,
"Sir," said I, "or Madam, truly your forgiveness I implore;
But the fact is I was napping, and so gently you came rapping,
And so faintly you came tapping, tapping at my chamber door,
That I scarce was sure I heard you"—here I opened wide the door;—
  Darkness there and nothing more.

Deep into that darkness peering, long I stood there wondering, fearing,
Doubting, dreaming dreams no mortal ever dared to dream before;
But the silence was unbroken, and the stillness gave no token,
And the only word there spoken was the whispered word, "Lenore?"
This I whispered, and an echo murmured back the word, "Lenore!"—
  Merely this and nothing more.

(continued next page)

Back into the chamber turning, all my soul within me burning,
Soon again I heard a tapping somewhat louder than before.
"Surely," said I, "surely that is something at my window lattice;
Let me see, then, what thereat is, and this mystery explore—
Let my heart be still a moment and this mystery explore;—
        'Tis the wind and nothing more!"

Open here I flung the shutter, when, with many a flirt and flutter,
In there stepped a stately Raven of the saintly days of yore;
Not the least obeisance made he; not a minute stopped or stayed he;
But, with mien of lord or lady, perched above my chamber door—
Perched upon a bust of Pallas just above my chamber door—
        Perched, and sat, and nothing more.

Then this ebony bird beguiling my sad fancy into smiling,
By the grave and stern decorum of the countenance it wore,
"Though thy crest be shorn and shaven, thou," I said, "art sure no craven,
Ghastly grim and ancient Raven wandering from the Nightly shore—
Tell me what thy lordly name is on the Night's Plutonian shore!"
        Quoth the Raven "Nevermore."

Much I marvelled this ungainly fowl to hear discourse so plainly,
Though its answer little meaning—little relevancy bore;
For we cannot help agreeing that no living human being
Ever yet was blest with seeing bird above his chamber door—
Bird or beast upon the sculptured bust above his chamber door,
        With such name as "Nevermore."

But the Raven, sitting lonely on the placid bust, spoke only
That one word, as if his soul in that one word he did outpour.
Nothing further then he uttered—not a feather then he fluttered—
Till I scarcely more than muttered "Other friends have flown before—
On the morrow *he* will leave me, as my hopes have flown before."
        Then the bird said "Nevermore."

(continued next page)

Startled at the stillness broken by reply so aptly spoken,
"Doubtless," said I, "what it utters is its only stock and store
Caught from some unhappy master whom unmerciful Disaster
Followed fast and followed faster till his songs one burden bore—
Till the dirges of his Hope that melancholy burden bore
      Of 'Never—nevermore.'"

But the Raven still beguiling my sad fancy into smiling,
Straight I wheeled a cushioned seat in front of bird, and bust and door;
Then, upon the velvet sinking, I betook myself to linking
Fancy unto fancy, thinking what this ominous bird of yore—
What this grim, ungainly, ghastly, gaunt and ominous bird of yore
      Meant in croaking "Nevermore."

This I sat engaged in guessing, but no syllable expressing
To the fowl whose fiery eyes now burned into my bosom's core;
This and more I sat divining, with my head at ease reclining
On the cushion's velvet lining that the lamp-light gloated o'er,
But whose velvet violet lining with the lamp-light gloating o'er,
      She shall press, ah, nevermore!

Then, methought, the air grew denser, perfumed from an unseen censer
Swung by Seraphim whose foot-falls tinkled on the tufted floor.
"Wretch," I cried, "thy God hath lent thee—by these angels he hath sent thee
Respite—respite and nepenthe, from thy memories of Lenore;
Quaff, oh quaff this kind nepenthe and forget this lost Lenore!"
      Quoth the Raven "Nevermore."

"Prophet!" said I, "thing of evil!—prophet still, if bird or devil!—
Whether Tempter sent, or whether tempest tossed thee here ashore,
Desolate yet all undaunted, on this desert land enchanted—
On this home by Horror haunted—tell me truly, I implore—
Is there—is there balm in Gilead?—tell me—tell me, I implore!"
      Quoth the Raven "Nevermore."

(continued next page)

"Prophet!" said I, "thing of evil—prophet still, if bird or devil!
By that Heaven that bends above us—by that God we both adore—
Tell this soul with sorrow laden if, within the distant Aidenn,
It shall clasp a sainted maiden whom the angels name Lenore—
Clasp a rare and radiant maiden whom the angels name Lenore."
        Quoth the Raven "Nevermore."

"Be that word our sign in parting, bird or fiend!" I shrieked, upstarting—
"Get thee back into the tempest and the Night's Plutonian shore!
Leave no black plume as a token of that lie thy soul hath spoken!
Leave my loneliness unbroken!—quit the bust above my door!
Take thy beak from out my heart, and take thy form from off my door!"
        Quoth the Raven "Nevermore."

And the Raven, never flitting, still is sitting, *still* is sitting
On the pallid bust of Pallas just above my chamber door;
And his eyes have all the seeming of a demon's that is dreaming,
And the lamp-light o'er him streaming throws his shadow on the floor;
And my soul from out that shadow that lies floating on the floor
        Shall be lifted—nevermore!

"Ode on Solitude" by Alexander Pope

Happy the man, whose wish and care
   A few paternal acres bound,
Content to breathe his native air,
      In his own ground.

Whose herds with milk, whose fields with bread,
   Whose flocks supply him with attire,
Whose trees in summer yield him shade,
      In winter fire.

Blest, who can unconcernedly find
   Hours, days, and years slide soft away,
In health of body, peace of mind,
      Quiet by day,

Sound sleep by night; study and ease,
   Together mixed; sweet recreation;
And innocence, which most does please,
      With meditation.

Thus let me live, unseen, unknown;
   Thus unlamented let me die;
Steal from the world, and not a stone
      Tell where I lie.

"Know Thyself" by Alexander Pope

Know then thyself, presume not God to scan;
The proper study of mankind is Man.
Placed on this isthmus of a middle state,
A being darkly wise and rudely great:
With too much knowledge for the Sceptic side,
With too much weakness for the Stoic's pride,
He hangs between; in doubt to act or rest,
In doubt to deem himself a God or Beast,
In doubt his mind or body to prefer;
Born but to die, and reasoning but to err;
Alike in ignorance, his reason such
Whether he thinks too little or too much:
Chaos of thought and passion, all confused;
Still by himself abused, or disabused;
Created half to rise and half to fall;
Great lord of all things, yet a prey to all;
Sole judge of truth, in endless error hurled:
The glory, jest, and riddle of the world!

"Pibroch of Dunald Dhu (The pipe-summons of Donald the Black or Gathering Song of Donald the Black)" by Sir Walter Scott

Pibroch of Donuil Dhu,
  Pibroch of Donuil,
Wake thy wild voice anew,
  Summon Clan Conuil.
Come away, come away,
  Hark to the summons!
Come in your war array,
  Gentles and commons.
Come from deep glen, and
  From mountain so rocky,
The war-pipe and pennon
  Are at Inverlochy.
Come every hill-plaid, and
  True heart that wears one,
Come every steel blade, and
  Strong hand that bears one.
Leave untended the herd,
  The flock without shelter;
Leave the corpse uninterr'd,
  The bride at the altar;

Leave the deer, leave the steer,
  Leave nets and barges:
Come with your fighting gear,
  Broadswords and targes.
Come as the winds come, when
  Forests are rended;
Come as the waves come, when
  Navies are stranded:
Faster come, faster come,
  Faster and faster,
Chief, vassal, page and groom,
  Tenant and master.
Fast they come, fast they come;
  See how they gather!
Wide waves the eagle plume,
  Blended with heather.
Cast your plaids, draw your blades,
  Forward each man set!
Pibroch of Donuil Dhu,
  Knell for the onset!

"Blow, Bugle, Blow" by Alfred, Lord Tennyson

The splendour falls on castle walls
    And snowy summits old in story:
The long light shakes across the lakes,
    And the wild cataract leaps in glory.
Blow, bugle, blow, set the wild echoes flying,
Blow, bugle; answer, echoes, dying, dying, dying.

O hark, O hear! how thin and clear,
    And thinner, clearer, farther going!
O sweet and far from cliff and scar
    The horns of Elfland faintly blowing!
Blow, let us hear the purple-glens replying:
Blow, bugle; answer, echoes, dying, dying, dying.

O love, they die in yon rich sky,
    They faint on hill or field or river:
Our echoes roll from soul to soul,
    And grow for ever and for ever.
Blow, bugle, blow, set the wild echoes flying,
And answer, echoes, answer, dying, dying, dying.

"On The Banks O' Deer Crick" by James Whitcomb Riley

On the banks o' Deer Crick! There's the place fer me!--
Worter slidin' past ye jes as clair as it kin be:--
See yer shadder in it, and the shadder o' the sky,
And the shadder o' the buzzard as he goes a-lazein' by;
Shadder o' the pizen-vines, and shadder o' the trees--
And I purt'-nigh said the shadder o' the sunshine and the breeze!
Well--I never seen the ocean ner I never seen the sea:
On the banks o' Deer Crick's grand enough fer me!

On the banks o' Deer Crick--mild er two from town--
'Long up where the mill-race comes a-loafin' down,--
Like to git up in there--'mongst the sycamores--
And watch the worter at the dam, a-frothin' as she pours:
Crawl out on some old log, with my hook and line,
Where the fish is jes so thick you kin see 'em shine
As they flicker round yer bait, _coaxin_' you to jerk,
Tel yer tired ketchin' of 'em, mighty nigh, as _work_!

On the banks o' Deer Crick!--Allus my delight
Jes to be around there--take it day er night!--
Watch the snipes and killdees foolin' half the day--
Er these-'ere little worter-bugs skootin' ever'way!--
Snakefeeders glancin' round, er dartin' out o' sight;
And dew-fall, and bullfrogs, and lightnin'-bugs at night--
Stars up through the tree-tops--er in the crick below,--
And smell o' mussrat through the dark clean from the old b'y-o!

Er take a tromp, some Sund'y, say, 'way up to 'Johnson's Hole,'
And find where he's had a fire, and hid his fishin' pole;
Have yer 'dog-leg,' with ye and yer pipe and 'cut-and-dry'--
Pocketful o' corn-bred, and slug er two o' rye,--
Soak yer hide in sunshine and waller in the shade--
Like the Good Book tells us--'where there're none to make afraid!'
Well!--I never seen the ocean ner I never seen the sea--
On the banks o' Deer Crick's grand enough fer me!

"Homo sapiens" by John Wilmot

Were I (who to my cost already am
One of those strange, prodigious creatures, man)
A spirit free to choose, for my own share,
What case of flesh and blood I pleased to wear,
I'd be a dog, a monkey, or a bear,
Or anything but that vain animal
Who is so proud of being rational.
The senses are too gross, and he'll contrive
A sixth, to contradict the other five,
And before certain instinct, will prefer
Reason, which fifty times for one does err ;
Reason, an ignis fatuus in the mind,
Which, leaving light of nature, sense, behind,
Pathless and dangerous wandering ways it takes
Through error's fenny bogs and thorny brakes ;
Whilst the misguided follower climbs with pain
Mountains of whimseys, heaped in his own brain ;
Stumbling from thought to thought, falls headlong down
Into doubt's boundless sea, where, like to drown,
Books bear him up awhile, and make him try
To swim with bladders of philosophy ;
In hopes still to o'ertake the escaping light,
The vapour dances in his dazzling sight
Till, spent, it leaves him to eternal night.
Then old age and experience, hand in hand,
Lead him to death, and make him understand,
After a search so painful and so long,
That all his life he has been in the wrong.
Huddled in dirt the reasoning engine lies,
Who was so proud, so witty, and so wise.

"The Tyger" by William Blake

Tyger Tyger, burning bright,
In the forests of the night;
What immortal hand or eye,
Could frame thy fearful symmetry?

In what distant deeps or skies,
Burnt the fire of thine eyes?
On what wings dare he aspire?
What the hand, dare seize the fire?

And what shoulder, & what art,
Could twist the sinews of thy heart?
And when thy heart began to beat,
What dread hand? & what dread feet?

What the hammer? what the chain,
In what furnace was thy brain?
What the anvil? what dread grasp,
Dare its deadly terrors clasp!

When the stars threw down their spears
And water'd heaven with their tears:
Did he smile his work to see?
Did he who made the Lamb make thee?

Tyger Tyger burning bright,
In the forests of the night:
What immortal hand or eye,
Dare frame thy fearful symmetry?

"Fragment from 'Auguries of Innocence'" by William Blake

To see a World in a Grain of Sand
And a Heaven in a Wild Flower,
Hold Infinity in the palm of your hand
And Eternity in an hour.

"Sea Fever" by John Masefield

I must go down to the seas again, to the lonely sea and the sky,
And all I ask is a tall ship and a star to steer her by;
And the wheel's kick and the wind's song and the white sail's shaking,
And a grey mist on the sea's face, and a grey dawn breaking.

I must go down to the seas again, for the call of the running tide
Is a wild call and a clear call that may not be denied;
And all I ask is a windy day with the white clouds flying,
And the flung spray and the blown spume, and the sea-gulls crying.

I must go down to the seas again, to the vagrant gypsy life,
To the gull's way and the whale's way where the wind's like a whetted knife;
And all I ask is a merry yarn from a laughing fellow-rover,
And quiet sleep and a sweet dream when the long trick's over.

"A Dream Within a Dream" by Edgar Allan Poe

Take this kiss upon the brow!
And, in parting from you now,
Thus much let me avow —
You are not wrong, who deem
That my days have been a dream;
Yet if hope has flown away
In a night, or in a day,
In a vision, or in none,
Is it therefore the less *gone*?
All that we see or seem
Is but a dream within a dream.

I stand amid the roar
Of a surf-tormented shore,
And I hold within my hand
Grains of the golden sand —
How few! yet how they creep
Through my fingers to the deep,
While I weep — while I weep!
O God! Can I not grasp
Them with a tighter clasp?
O God! can I not save
One from the pitiless wave?
Is *all* that we see or seem
But a dream within a dream?

"Renascence" by Edna St. Vincent Millay

ALL I could see from where I stood
Was three long mountains and a wood;
I turned and looked the other way,
And saw three islands in a bay.
So with my eyes I traced the line
Of the horizon, thin and fine,
Straight around till I was come
Back to where I'd started from;
And all I saw from where I stood
Was three long mountains and a wood.
Over these things I could not see:
These were the things that bounded me;
And I could touch them with my hand,
Almost, I thought, from where I stand.
And all at once things seemed so small
My breath came short, and scarce at all.
But, sure, the sky is big, I said;
Miles and miles above my head;
So here upon my back I'll lie
And look my fill into the sky.
And so I looked, and, after all,
The sky was not so very tall.
The sky, I said, must somewhere stop,
And—sure enough!—I see the top!
The sky, I thought, is not so grand;
I 'most could touch it with my hand!
And reaching up my hand to try,
I screamed to feel it touch the sky.
I screamed, and—lo!—Infinity
Came down and settled over me;
Forced back my scream into my chest,
Bent back my arm upon my breast,
And, pressing of the Undefined
The definition on my mind,
Held up before my eyes a glass
Through which my shrinking sight did pass

(continued next page)

Until it seemed I must behold
Immensity made manifold;
Whispered to me a word whose sound
Deafened the air for worlds around,
And brought unmuffled to my ears
The gossiping of friendly spheres,
The creaking of the tented sky,
The ticking of Eternity.
I saw and heard and knew at last
The How and Why of all things, past,
And present, and forevermore.
The Universe, cleft to the core,
Lay open to my probing sense
That, sick'ning, I would fain pluck thence
But could not,—nay! But needs must suck
At the great wound, and could not pluck
My lips away till I had drawn
All venom out.—Ah, fearful pawn!
For my omniscience paid I toll
In infinite remorse of soul.
All sin was of my sinning, all
Atoning mine, and mine the gall
Of all regret. Mine was the weight
Of every brooded wrong, the hate
That stood behind each envious thrust,
Mine every greed, mine every lust.
And all the while for every grief,
Each suffering, I craved relief
With individual desire,—
Craved all in vain! And felt fierce fire
About a thousand people crawl;
Perished with each,—then mourned for all!
A man was starving in Capri;
He moved his eyes and looked at me;
I felt his gaze, I heard his moan,
And knew his hunger as my own.
I saw at sea a great fog bank
Between two ships that struck and sank;

(continued next page)

A thousand screams the heavens smote;
And every scream tore through my throat.
No hurt I did not feel, no death
That was not mine; mine each last breath
That, crying, met an answering cry
From the compassion that was I.
All suffering mine, and mine its rod;
Mine, pity like the pity of God.
Ah, awful weight! Infinity
Pressed down upon the finite Me!
My anguished spirit, like a bird,
Beating against my lips I heard;
Yet lay the weight so close about
There was no room for it without.
And so beneath the weight lay I
And suffered death, but could not die.

Long had I lain thus, craving death,
When quietly the earth beneath
Gave way, and inch by inch, so great
At last had grown the crushing weight,
Into the earth I sank till I
Full six feet under ground did lie,
And sank no more,—there is no weight
Can follow here, however great.
From off my breast I felt it roll,
And as it went my tortured soul
Burst forth and fled in such a gust
That all about me swirled the dust.

Deep in the earth I rested now;
Cool is its hand upon the brow
And soft its breast beneath the head
Of one who is so gladly dead.
And all at once, and over all
The pitying rain began to fall;
I lay and heard each pattering hoof
Upon my lowly, thatchèd roof,

(continued next page)

And seemed to love the sound far more
Than ever I had done before.
For rain it hath a friendly sound
To one who's six feet under ground;
And scarce the friendly voice or face:
A grave is such a quiet place.

The rain, I said, is kind to come
And speak to me in my new home.
I would I were alive again
To kiss the fingers of the rain,
To drink into my eyes the shine
Of every slanting silver line,
To catch the freshened, fragrant breeze
From drenched and dripping apple-trees.
For soon the shower will be done,
And then the broad face of the sun
Will laugh above the rain-soaked earth
Until the world with answering mirth
Shakes joyously, and each round drop
Rolls, twinkling, from its grass-blade top.
How can I bear it; buried here,
While overhead the sky grows clear
And blue again after the storm?
O, multi-colored, multiform,
Beloved beauty over me,
That I shall never, never see
Again! Spring-silver, autumn-gold,
That I shall never more behold!
Sleeping your myriad magics through,
Close-sepulchred away from you!
O God, I cried, give me new birth,
And put me back upon the earth!
Upset each cloud's gigantic gourd
And let the heavy rain, down-poured
In one big torrent, set me free,
Washing my grave away from me!

(continued next page)

I ceased; and through the breathless hush
That answered me, the far-off rush
Of herald wings came whispering
Like music down the vibrant string
Of my ascending prayer, and—crash!
Before the wild wind's whistling lash
The startled storm-clouds reared on high
And plunged in terror down the sky,
And the big rain in one black wave
Fell from the sky and struck my grave.
I know not how such things can be;
I only know there came to me
A fragrance such as never clings
To aught save happy living things;
A sound as of some joyous elf
Singing sweet songs to please himself,
And, through and over everything,
A sense of glad awakening.
The grass, a-tiptoe at my ear,
Whispering to me I could hear;
I felt the rain's cool finger-tips
Brushed tenderly across my lips,
Laid gently on my sealèd sight,
And all at once the heavy night
Fell from my eyes and I could see,—
A drenched and dripping apple-tree,
A last long line of silver rain,
A sky grown clear and blue again.
And as I looked a quickening gust
Of wind blew up to me and thrust
Into my face a miracle
Of orchard-breath, and with the smell,—
I know not how such things can be!—
I breathed my soul back into me.
Ah! Up then from the ground sprang I
And hailed the earth with such a cry
As is not heard save from a man
Who has been dead, and lives again.

(continued next page)

About the trees my arms I wound;
Like one gone mad I hugged the ground;
I raised my quivering arms on high;
I laughed and laughed into the sky,
Till at my throat a strangling sob
Caught fiercely, and a great heart-throb
Sent instant tears into my eyes;
O God, I cried, no dark disguise
Can e'er hereafter hide from me
Thy radiant identity!
Thou canst not move across the grass
But my quick eyes will see Thee pass,
Nor speak, however silently,
But my hushed voice will answer Thee.
I know the path that tells Thy way
Through the cool eve of every day;
God, I can push the grass apart
And lay my finger on Thy heart!

The world stands out on either side
No wider than the heart is wide;
Above the world is stretched the sky,—
No higher than the soul is high.
The heart can push the sea and land
Farther away on either hand;
The soul can split the sky in two,
And let the face of God shine through.
But East and West will pinch the heart
That can not keep them pushed apart;
And he whose soul is flat—the sky
Will cave in on him by and by.

"The Road Not Taken" by Robert Frost

TWO roads diverged in a yellow wood,
And sorry I could not travel both
And be one traveler, long I stood
And looked down one as far as I could
To where it bent in the undergrowth;

Then took the other, as just as fair,
And having perhaps the better claim
Because it was grassy and wanted wear;
Though as for that, the passing there
Had worn them really about the same,

And both that morning equally lay
In leaves no step had trodden black.

Oh, I marked the first for another day!
Yet knowing how way leads on to way
I doubted if I should ever come back.

I shall be telling this with a sigh
Somewhere ages and ages hence:
Two roads diverged in a wood, and I,
I took the one less traveled by,
And that has made all the difference.

"Stopping by Woods On A Snowy Evening" by Robert Frost

Whose woods these are I think I know.
His house is in the village though;
He will not see me stopping here
To watch his woods fill up with snow.

My little horse must think it queer
To stop without a farmhouse near
Between the woods and frozen lake
The darkest evening of the year.

He gives his harness bells a shake
To ask if there is some mistake.
The only other sound's the sweep
Of easy wind and downy flake.

The woods are lovely, dark and deep.
But I have promises to keep,
And miles to go before I sleep,
And miles to go before I sleep.

"Tomorrow, At Dawn" by Victor Hugo

Tomorrow, at dawn, at the hour when the countryside whitens,
I will set out. You see, I know that you wait for me.
I will go by the forest, I will go by the mountain.
I can no longer remain far from you.

I will walk with my eyes fixed on my thoughts,
Seeing nothing of outdoors, hearing no noise
Alone, unknown, my back curved, my hands crossed,
Sorrowed, and the day for me will be as the night.

I will not look at the gold of evening which falls,
Nor the distant sails going down towards Harfleur,
And when I arrive, I will place on your tomb
A bouquet of green holly and of flowering heather.

"The Bells" by Edgar Allan Poe

I.

Hear the sledges with the bells—
Silver bells!
What a world of merriment their melody foretells!
How they tinkle, tinkle, tinkle,
In the icy air of night!
While the stars that oversprinkle
All the heavens, seem to twinkle
With a crystalline delight;
Keeping time, time, time,
In a sort of Runic rhyme,
To the tintinabulation that so musically wells
From the bells, bells, bells, bells,
Bells, bells, bells—
From the jingling and the tinkling of the bells.

II.

Hear the mellow wedding bells,
Golden bells!
What a world of happiness their harmony foretells!
Through the balmy air of night
How they ring out their delight!
From the molten-golden notes,
And all in tune,
What a liquid ditty floats
To the turtle-dove that listens, while she gloats
On the moon!
Oh, from out the sounding cells,
What a gush of euphony voluminously wells!
How it swells!
How it dwells
On the Future! how it tells
Of the rapture that impels
To the swinging and the ringing
Of the bells, bells, bells,
Of the bells, bells, bells, bells,
Bells, bells, bells—
To the rhyming and the chiming of the bells!

(continued next page)

III.

Hear the loud alarum bells—
Brazen bells!
What tale of terror, now, their turbulency tells!
In the startled ear of night
How they scream out their affright!
Too much horrified to speak,
They can only shriek, shriek,
Out of tune,
In a clamorous appealing to the mercy of the fire,
In a mad expostulation with the deaf and frantic fire,
Leaping higher, higher, higher,
With a desperate desire,
And a resolute endeavor
Now—now to sit or never,
By the side of the pale-faced moon.
Oh, the bells, bells, bells!
What a tale their terror tells
Of Despair!
How they clang, and clash, and roar!
What a horror they outpour
On the bosom of the palpitating air!
Yet the ear it fully knows,
By the twanging,
And the clanging,
How the danger ebbs and flows;
Yet the ear distinctly tells,
In the jangling,
And the wrangling.
How the danger sinks and swells,
By the sinking or the swelling in the anger of the bells—
Of the bells—
Of the bells, bells, bells, bells,
Bells, bells, bells—
In the clamor and the clangor of the bells!

IV.

Hear the tolling of the bells—
Iron bells!
What a world of solemn thought their monody compels!

(continued next page)

In the silence of the night,
How we shiver with affright
At the melancholy menace of their tone!
For every sound that floats
From the rust within their throats
Is a groan.
And the people—ah, the people—
They that dwell up in the steeple,
All alone,
And who tolling, tolling, tolling,
In that muffled monotone,
Feel a glory in so rolling
On the human heart a stone—
They are neither man nor woman—
They are neither brute nor human—
They are Ghouls:
And their king it is who tolls;
And he rolls, rolls, rolls,
Rolls
A pæan from the bells!
And his merry bosom swells
With the pæan of the bells!
And he dances, and he yells;
Keeping time, time, time,
In a sort of Runic rhyme,
To the pæan of the bells—
Of the bells:
Keeping time, time, time,
In a sort of Runic rhyme,
To the throbbing of the bells—
Of the bells, bells, bells—
To the sobbing of the bells;
Keeping time, time, time,
As he knells, knells, knells,
In a happy Runic rhyme,
To the rolling of the bells—
Of the bells, bells, bells—
To the tolling of the bells,
Of the bells, bells, bells, bells—
Bells, bells, bells—
To the moaning and the groaning of the bells.

"Eletelephony" by Laura Elizabeth Richards

Once there was an elephant,
Who tried to use the telephant—
No! No! I mean an elephone
Who tried to use the telephone—
(Dear me! I am not certain quite
That even now I've got it right.)
Howe'er it was, he got his trunk
Entangled in the telephunk;
The more he tried to get it free,
The louder buzzed the telephee—
(I fear I'd better drop the song
Of elephop and telephong!)

"A Poison Tree" by William Blake

I was angry with my friend:
I told my wrath, my wrath did end.
I was angry with my foe:
I told it not, my wrath did grow.

And I watered it in fears
Night and morning with my tears,
And I sunned it with smiles
And with soft deceitful wiles.

And it grew both day and night,
Till it bore an apple bright,
And my foe beheld it shine,
And he knew that it was mine,--

And into my garden stole
When the night had veiled the pole;
In the morning, glad, I see
My foe outstretched beneath the tree.

"Though Ye Suppose" by John Skelton

Though ye suppose all jeopardies are past,
   And all is done ye looked for before,
Ware yet, I rede you, of Fortune's double cast,
   For one false point she is wont to keep in store,
   And under the fell oft festered is the sore:
That when ye think all danger for to pass
Ware of the lizard lieth lurking in the grass.

"So we'll go no more a roving" by George Gordon, Lord Byron

So, we'll go no more a roving
   So late into the night,
Though the heart be still as loving,
   And the moon be still as bright.

For the sword outwears its sheath,
   And the soul wears out the breast,
And the heart must pause to breathe,
   And love itself have rest.

Though the night was made for loving,
   And the day returns too soon,
Yet we'll go no more a roving
   By the light of the moon.

"She Walks in Beauty" by George Gordon, Lord Byron

I.

She walks in beauty, like the night
   Of cloudless climes and starry skies;
And all that's best of dark and bright
   Meet in her aspect and her eyes:
Thus mellowed to that tender light
   Which heaven to gaudy day denies.

II.

One shade the more, one ray the less,
   Had half impaired the nameless grace
Which waves in every raven tress,
   Or softly lightens o'er her face;
Where thoughts serenely sweet express
   How pure, how dear their dwelling place.

III.

And on that cheek, and o'er that brow,
   So soft, so calm, yet eloquent,
The smiles that win, the tints that glow,
   But tell of days in goodness spent,
A mind at peace with all below,
   A heart whose love is innocent!

"To Lucasta, on Going to the Wars" by Richard Lovelace

Tell me not, Sweet, I am unkind,
  That from the nunnery
Of thy chaste breast and quiet mind
  To war and arms I fly.

True, a new mistress now I chase,
  The first foe in the field;
And with a stronger faith embrace
  A sword, a horse, a shield.

Yet this inconstancy is such
  As thou too shalt adore;
I could not love thee, Dear, so much,
  Loved I not Honour more.

"Mutability" by Percy Bysshe Shelley

We are as clouds that veil the midnight moon;
  How restlessly they speed, and gleam, and quiver,
Streaking the darkness radiantly!—yet soon
  Night closes round, and they are lost for ever:

Or like forgotten lyres, whose dissonant strings
  Give various response to each varying blast,
To whose frail frame no second motion brings
  One mood or modulation like the last.

We rest.—A dream has power to poison sleep;
  We rise.—One wandering thought pollutes the day;
We feel, conceive or reason, laugh or weep;
  Embrace fond woe, or cast our cares away:

It is the same!—For, be it joy or sorrow,
  The path of its departure still is free:
Man's yesterday may ne'er be like his morrow;
  Nought may endure but Mutability.

"A Moment of Love" by Carl Scott Harker

I'd like to know
What's going on in your mind,
Take the time
To say what's percolating.

I'd like to see
What's flowing through your heart,
Won't you start
Communicating.

Then we will say
That it's okay
And share an orange,
Our eyes will meet
How sweet,
In understanding.

The wind will blow
The sun will shine,
We'll enter a whirlpool in time
And know the power of the weather:

Constant change, constant change, constant change.

"The Swing" by Robert Louis Stevenson

How do you like to go up in a swing,
      Up in the air so blue?
Oh, I do think it the pleasantest thing
      Ever a child can do!

Up in the air and over the wall,
      Till I can see so wide,
River and trees and cattle and all
      Over the countryside—

Till I look down on the garden green,
      Down on the roof so brown—
Up in the air I go flying again,
      Up in the air and down!

"My Shadow" by Robert Louis Stevenson

I have a little shadow that goes in and out with me,
And what can be the use of him is more than I can see.
He is very, very like me from the heels up to the head;
And I see him jump before me, when I jump into my bed.

The funniest thing about him is the way he likes to grow—
Not at all like proper children, which is always very slow;
For he sometimes shoots up taller like an India-rubber ball,
And he sometimes gets so little that there's none of him at all.

He hasn't got a notion of how children ought to play,
And can only make a fool of me in every sort of way.
He stays so close beside me, he's a coward you can see;
I'd think shame to stick to nursie as that shadow sticks to me!

One morning, very early, before the sun was up,
I rose and found the shining dew on every buttercup;
But my lazy little shadow, like an arrant sleepy-head,
Had stayed at home behind me and was fast asleep in bed.

"Clouds" by Christina Rossetti

White sheep, white sheep,
On a blue hill,
When the wind stops,
You all stand still.

When the wind blows,
You walk away slow.
White sheep, white sheep,
Where do you go?

"Afternoon on a Hill" by Edna St. Vincent Millay

I will be the gladdest thing
Under the sun!
I will touch a hundred flowers
And not pick one.
I will look at cliffs and clouds
With quiet eyes,
Watch the wind bow down the grass,
And the grass rise.
And when lights begin to show
Up from the town,
I will mark which must be mine,
And then start down!

"Buffalo Bill's" by e. e. cummings (Edward Estlin Cummings)

Buffalo Bill's
defunct
      who used to
      ride a watersmooth-silver
                  stallion
and break onetwothreefourfive pigeonsjustlikethat
                            Jesus

he was a handsome man
                  and what i want to know is
how do you like your blueeyed boy
Mister Death

"Auld Lang Syne (Times Long Ago)" by Robert Burns (Modern Version)

Should old acquaintance be forgot,
    And never brought to mind?
Should old acquaintance be forgot,
    And times long ago!

    Chorus:
    For times long ago, my dear,
    For times long ago.
    We'll take a cup of kindness yet,
    For times long ago.

And surely ye'll be your pint ladle!
    And surely I'll be mine!
And we'll take a cup of kindness yet,
    For times long ago.

    Chorus:
    For times long ago, my dear,
    For times long ago.
    We'll take a cup of kindness yet,
    For times long ago.

We two have run about the hills,
    And pulled the flowers fine;
But we've wander'd many a weary step,
    Since times long ago.

    Chorus:
    For times long ago, my dear,
    For times long ago.
    We'll take a cup of kindness yet,
    For times long ago.

We two have paddled in the stream,
    From morning sun till dine;
But seas between us broad have roar'd
    Since times long go.

(continued next page)

Chorus:
For times long ago, my dear,
For times long ago.
We'll take a cup of kindness yet,
For times long ago.

And there's a hand, my trusty friend!
   And give a hand of thine!
And we'll take a drink of right good will,
   For times long ago.

Chorus:

For times long ago, my dear,
For times long ago.
We'll take a cup of kindness yet,
For times long ago.

...

"Auld Lang Syne" by Robert Burns (Original Version)

Should auld acquaintance be forgot,
   And never brought to mind?
Should auld acquaintance be forgot,
   And auld lang syne!

Chorus:
For auld lang syne, my dear,
For auld lang syne.
We'll tak a cup o' kindness yet,
For auld lang syne.

And surely ye'll be your pint stowp!
   And surely I'll be mine!
And we'll tak a cup o' kindness yet,
   For auld lang syne.

(continued next page)

Chorus:
For auld lang syne, my dear,
For auld lang syne.
We'll tak a cup o' kindness yet,
For auld lang syne.

We twa hae run about the braes,
    And pou'd the gowans fine;
But we've wander'd mony a weary fit,
    Sin' auld lang syne.

Chorus:
For auld lang syne, my dear,
For auld lang syne.
We'll tak a cup o' kindness yet,
For auld lang syne.

We twa hae paidl'd in the burn,
    Frae morning sun till dine;
But seas between us braid hae roar'd
    Sin' auld lang syne.

Chorus:
For auld lang syne, my dear,
For auld lang syne.
We'll tak a cup o' kindness yet,
For auld lang syne.

And there's a hand, my trusty fere!
    And gie's a hand o' thine!
And we'll tak a right gude-willie waught,
    For auld lang syne.

Chorus:

For auld lang syne, my dear,
For auld lang syne.
We'll tak a cup o' kindness yet,
For auld lang syne.

"Travelling" by William Wordsworth

This is the spot: —how mildly does the sun
Shine in between the fading leaves! the air
In the habitual silence of this wood
Is more than silent: and this bed of heath,
Where shall we find so sweet a resting-place?
Come! —let me see thee sink into a dream
Of quiet thoughts, —protracted till thine eye
Be calm as water when the winds are gone
And no one can tell whither. —my sweet friend!
We two have had such happy hours together
That my heart melts in me to think of it.

NOTES ON THE POEMS

1. **"Ozymandias"** by Percy Bysshe Shelley. Poets are synthesizers of the topics of the their days. At the time this poem was written, the science of archeology and its findings were much talked about by the educated. It is not surprising, then, for Shelley to use archeology as a framework for this poem.

2. **"You are old, Father William"** by Lewis Carroll. This is a humorous poem where youth and old age banter. But after reading this poem as a child – Father William became a "goal model" for me - to become stronger and wiser the older I get.

3. **"The Owl and the Pussycat"** by Edward Lear. This is, ostensibly, a children's poem. But for me it is a great love poem and delight to say out loud. By the end of the poem and its repetition of the words at the end of each stanza – how can you not be smiling?

4. **"No Man is an Island"** – John Donne. While Donne wrote other poems, of course, this is the one poem of his that will still be read a thousand years from now. It is so fundamental in subject. And so concretely expressed. Today, we are connected by the Internet, but I think we are even more connected by the local grocery store where food from around the world is available to me and to you every day. We are so interdependent.

5. **"The Charge of the Light Brigade"** by Alfred, Lord Tennyson. This poem is about the bravery of those who knowingly face death. It is also a public relations poem highlighting heroism in the thrill of battle while downplaying needless death due to a poor military decision. While it is a rollicking poem, I can only hope that soon such words as *"Theirs not to reason why, Theirs but to do and die."* will refer to Virtual Reality Wars where no one is really injured and the winner has the honor of paying the annual budget for the Moon Colony or some other worthwhile future cause.

6. **"Kubla Khan"** by Samuel Taylor Coleridge. If you have a favorite song, or vista or piece of art that you never get tired of – that is what this poem is to me. Every word in it is a treasure, every image is ever new. You can pick out lines at random *"Then reached the caverns measureless to man,"* or *"A miracle of rare device."* or *"For he on honey-dew hath fed,"* that beg to be spoken. The poem is a vision that one can never exactly grasp or ever stop reveling in what you can grasp.

7. **"Ulysses"** by Alfred Lord Tennyson. Based upon Greek poet Homer's story of Odysseus (Greek) or Ulysses (Roman), Tennyson had a lot of good material to work with when composing this poem. Still the amount of themes he touches on in a relatively small number of lines is masterful and this maybe Tennyson's masterpiece. While our personal adventures maybe small, and the details vary greatly from the life of Ulysses, I cannot think of a better road map to living life to the fullest than the poem's description of the ancient hero's life and motivations.

8. **"In Flanders Field"** by John McCrae. This poem came out of World War One.

9. **"Columbus"** by Joaquin Miller (1892). Setting aside the current debate of whether Columbus was a monster or a hero or somewhere in between, this poem celebrates characteristics that we all should admire – courage and persistence.

10. **"Jabberwocky"** by Lewis Carroll. You will not find most of the words in this poem in the dictionary – as such words are all made up. But it doesn't matter if you have never heard of "borogoves" or what it mean when "mome raths outgrabe," because the words of the poem, that we do understand, create sense in the nonsense words. Besides I love saying "snicker-snack" and "frabjous day!" This poem's collection of created phrases by Carroll are likely to hold the record for inspiring the titles of other written works.

11. **"Some One"** by Walter de la Mare. This poem is about one of life's little mysteries – who was the visitor we missed? Even with today's interconnectedness, a knock on the door can be missed, even phone calls can stop ringing without leaving a message, text or return number. This poem is a reminder that the unknown is with us even at mundane moments of the day.

12. **"Witches Spell Poem"** by William Shakespeare. This "poem" is part of the dialogue between three witches in Shakespeare's play "Macbeth." It contains some of the most easily remember lines in the Great Bard's plays.

13. **"On The Landing"** by Francis Bret Harte. This is a fun poem to read with someone else. Two small children give their opinion of their parents' party while watching for an upstairs landing. Bret Harte is perhaps more familiar to readers for his short stories usually with a Western theme.

14. **"A Red, Red Rose"** by Robert Burns. If there is a poem that can be said to represent what it means to be considered a *Romantic Poem*, this is the one. In a few lines, it expresses the best of what romantic love is. Here is a tip: Keep this poem handy to be used in a serious dating cycle. Or for that time, you are far away from your love and want to remind her how much you love her.

15. **"The Ballad of How MacPherson Held the Floor"** By Robert Service. This humorous Yukon ballad by Service is one of the longer poems I have selected for this book, but well worth the reading through. Keeping up the rhythm of the rhymed couplets is a delightful challenge as you read this poem out loud and enjoy the battle on the night of Saint Andrew's Ball.

16. **"I heard a Fly buzz - when I died"** - (591) by Emily Dickinson. In this poem, Emily Dickinson nicely captures one's last drop of perception on this side of the veil.

17. **"Rubáiyát of Omar Khayyám"** translated by Edward FitzGerald. There are many quatrains by Omar Khayyám translated by FitzGerald, these three are among the most well-known. You will be considered quite witty, if you use them in casual conversations.

Other authors have translated the Persian poet as well, Harold Lamb in his delightful biography entitled *Omar Khayyám,* translated several quatrains including this one:

"When Spring's bright magic on the meadow lies,
   With wine beside me I sit, to devise
   A love song for my houri, call me a dog
If I can spare a thought to Paradise."

18. **"To the Virgins, to Make Much of Time"** by Robert Herrick. In this age of longevity, it may seem old-fashioned to advise one to marry before the blush of youth disappears. And yet, time is fleeting and we should make the most of it, while we can.

19. **"Death and Life"** by Robert William Service. This amusing poem takes a basic event in life and tells its truth.

20. **"Annabel Lee"** by Edgar Allan Poe. This poem maybe about a great love and the madness that comes from loss and grief or maybe it is a ghost story or a curse or all of the above.

21. **"Sudden Light"** by Dante Gabriel Rossetti. Is this a poem of reincarnation? Or a time travel poem? Maybe it is a dream? Is time itself reshuffling? I can almost grasp what is going on, then it escapes me. But I certainly understand the fervent desire to be with my love one more day and more more night. I love the puzzle here.

22. **"Pippa's Song"** by Robert Browning. Every so often a moment comes and everything is just the way it is supposed to be.

23. **"The Raven"** by Edgar Allan Poe. This is an hypnotic poem - like a chant where the repetition of "Nevermore" and its rhymes push you onward and onward through the poem. One can say this is basically a poem about death, grief and depression where grief and depression and a little madness wins. But in reality, this poem is a literary masterpiece that transcends its theme.

24. **"Ode on Solitude"** by Alexander Pope. This poem reminds me of all the good people who do not need credit for the work they do, having learned that living life is reward enough.

25. **"Know Thyself"** by Alexander Pope. What a contradiction is humankind. A marvelous poem of contrasting elements.

26. **"Pibroch of Dunald Dhu"** by Sir Walter Scott. A Scottish cry to war and a poem that gives your lips and tongue a nice workout.

27. **"Blow, Bugle, Blow"** by Alfred, Lord Tennyson. This is a subtle poem about war. For the Bugles are calling for help from a distant battle field – where the soldiers and the people are dying. But the rich and powerful in their castles as lovely as Elfland ignore the distant cries for help...

28. **"On The Banks O' Deer Crick"** by James Whitcomb Riley. This is a dialect poem – with the voice and pronunciation of how simple folk may have talked a hundred years or more ago. It is also a Nature Poem – expressing the beauties and delights of a small splash of water through a small spill of land.

29. **"Homo sapiens"** by John Wilmot. Here is a poem about the "false promise" of reason. This reference might be lost on some readers, but I can hear the voice of Rod Sterling speaking this poem as an afterword to some "The Twilight Zone" TV tale about one man's ambitious folly.

30. **"The Tyger"** by William Blake. This famous poem is about creation. It asks the question of how any one or being can create such an awesome and fearsome creature as the tiger out of whole cloth?

This poem is also famous for having an example of an "Eye rhyme" - where two words look like they rhyme on paper, but their actual pronunciation does not rhyme. The two word in this poem are "eye" and " symme<u>try</u>." As you read this poem out loud, you will be tempted to rhyme eye and symmetry – resist the urge!

31. **"Fragment from 'Auguries of Innocence'"** by William Blake. This 4-line poem by William Blake is just a fragment from a larger poem – yet it is one of the most famous stanzas in all of poetrydom. Much like a Zen koan, these lines are worthy of much meditation. And, perhaps, this Blake fragment is what inspired the following poem by Robert Service...

"A Grain Of Sand" by Robert William Service

If starry space no limit knows

(continued next page)

And sun succeeds to sun,
There is no reason to suppose
Our earth the only one.
'Mid countless constellations cast
A million worlds may be,
With each a God to bless or blast
And steer to destiny.

Just think! A million gods or so
To guide each vital stream,
With over all to boss the show
A Deity supreme.
Such magnitudes oppress my mind;
From cosmic space it swings;
So ultimately glad to find
Relief in little things.

For look! Within my hollow hand,
While round the earth careens,
I hold a single grain of sand
And wonder what it means.
Ah! If I had the eyes to see,
And brain to understand,
I think Life's mystery might be
Solved in this grain of sand.

32. **"Sea Fever"** by John Masefield. This is a poem about yearning – for the seas and for days gone by. I can only hope that this voice in this poem was able to go sailing again.

33. **"A Dream Within a Dream"** by Edgar Allan Poe. What is reality? As time so swiftly slips by, one may wonder if my life is real?

This poem has been one of my greatest allies. When times have been rough, taking a moment to remind myself that this moment is just a "dream within a dream," helps.

One more question that I have trouble resolving in this poem, is those first two lines. Who is the "you" and where is he off to?

34. **"Renascence"** by Edna St. Vincent Millay. This is such a marvelous poem of couplets after couplets taking us through death into life again. I am reminded of the empath who most guard himself from feeling too much of the pain that exists almost everywhere and yet must also keep his barriers lowered enough to allow the beauty that is everywhere to come inside.

Millay with this poem gives us a chance to see the mystery behind the universe, if only for a moment.

35. **"The Road Not Taken"** by Robert Frost. When we are very young we do't realize that we are making choices, in young adulthood it still seems we can take all the choices. Then at some point, you discover that there is only one road to travel on and each choice makes all the difference.

36. **"Stopping by Woods On A Snowy Evening"** by Robert Frost. The greatness of the poet Frost, I think, is his ability to show something simple and reveal something so vastly fundamental.

37. **"Tomorrow, At Dawn"** by Victor Hugo. The end of the journey of this poem marks the anniversary of grief and death.

38. **"The Bells"** by Edgar Allan Poe. This is a great poem to read aloud. Its greatest difficulty is peaking too high, too early in this poem. Keeping your energy and voice in check is a hard to do, for each stanza pulses out with sound.

39. **"Eletelephony"** by Laura Elizabeth Richards. This poem is just amusing. Oh, how clever we can be twisting words in English.

40. **"A Poison Tree"** by William Blake. Two points: After the first couple of lines – there is no deep meaning to this poem. And, it is nice to give a listener a nice surprise at the end.

41. **"Though Ye Suppose"** by John Skelton. The language of this poem is an older version of English – as time has made its changes. Yet, the message of the poem is as timely today, as it was then.

42. **"So we'll go no more a roving"** by George Gordon, Lord Byron. Old age tends to keep one from doing what we did earlier in life. I am glad we live in a time where our medical technology makes it easier to "make love in the night," at an older age, than it otherwise might be.

43. **"She Walks in Beauty"** by George Gordon, Lord Byron. When I first read this poem, I thought that Lord Byron was just describing the beauty of a young woman – ands he still is. But now that I have had some years of experience, I realize he is also describing the beauty of goodness, itself. For, if I look wisely around me, I often see the beauty he describes in others regardless of the passing of many years.

44. **"To Lucasta, on Going to the Wars"** by Richard Lovelace. Honor is a pretty powerful excuse for going to war. And it is still used by militaries around the world. But I wonder with all the carnage wars have caused – and are still causing – what is the real cost of "honor?"

45. **"Mutability"** by Percy Bysshe Shelley. It is a marvel how much is put into such a small space of words. In support of the final message of this poem, I point out that our sun is orbiting the center of the galaxy and that our galaxy is both orbiting the center of the universe and fleeing it at the same time. So no matter how long humanity resides upon the Earth, we will never be in the same space, tomorrow, as we are today.

46. **"A Moment of Love"** by Carl Scott Harker. Yes, this is one of my poems – I figured that if the great film director Alfred Hitchcock could have cameos in his movies, I could do the same here. Of course, I do not count it as one of the 50 great poems to read out loud, as in the book's title, but I do hope you enjoy it.

47. **"The Swing"** by Robert Louis Stevenson. One of the things I miss from childhood is being on a swing. I still know how to swing, I just don't have the time anymore.

48. **"My Shadow"** by Robert Louis Stevenson. Our shadow is another thing that hold fascination for children, but, except for some horror stories, it is almost forgotten by adults. Perhaps, that is because we live in cities with large buildings that take away our shadows during the day.

49. **"Clouds"** by Christina Rossetti. This is the least complicated poem in this collection of great poetry to read out loud. Really, clouds that look like sheep: That is the poem. But this poem recalls an act I imagine everyone, everywhere has done – watch the clouds go by. And where do they go?

Of interest to those who are fans of Tin Pan Alley songwriter Hoagy Carmichael, he put a tune to the Rossetti poem and turned it into a song. You can hear Carmichael's version of "Clouds" on Youtube.com, here: https://www.youtube.com/results?search_query=Clouds+Hoagy+Carmichael .

50. **"Afternoon on a Hill"** by Edna St. Vincent Millay. Is this what people are talking about when they say they are going to take an afternoon off?

51. **"Buffalo Bill's"** by e. e. cummings (Edward Estlin Cummings). How cummings placed his words on the page is unique in style. But his visual cues are all the guide you need to make this an exciting poem to read out loud.

52-53. **"Auld Lang Syne (Times Long Ago)"** by Robert Burns (modern & original versions). Here is a poem/song that is heard once a year – but usually only partially. One rarely hears all the stanzas, nor do that many people know the meanings of some of the "Scottish words." Thus here are two versions. I think that "Times long ago" works as well as "Auld lang syne."

54. **"Travelling"** by William Wordsworth. The message of this poem is one I hope you have had with this book. That you have had "happy hours" taking this journey through what I think are some of the best poems ever written and some of the best poems to read aloud and to share with others.

AFTERWORD

Poets are inventors and engineers of words. Using allusions, imagery and connotations that are already inside the reader's mind, a poet creates a new adventure of unexpected emotions, laughter, images, ideas or new perspectives - and often a combination of all of these.

The best poetry is the shortest written way to go from A to B. What "A" is and what "B" is are unknown until you start and finish the poem. It is surprising, what you might find along the way.

Of course, you have noticed that there are more than 50 poems included in this book. I added a couple of extra poems, just in case you thought one or two of the poems were not great...

Aldouspi Publications Catalog

More Books by this Author

1. **100 Classic Poems to Read At Christmas Time: Traditional Christmas and Winter Poetry** – Great Christmas poems to exploring the various aspects of Christmas.

2. **The Case of the Missing Book: A Perry Mason Reading Guide** – Find all the Perry Mason novels in order of publication.

3. **The Light of Different Stars: A Jack Vance Book Guide** – Here is a reading guide in the order of publication of the science fiction, fantasy and mystery works of Jack Vance.

4. **The Farewell Kiss** – A comedic story/monologue based on the works of Edgar Allen Poe.

5. **Classic Fine Art Nudes: Volume One** – A collection of fine art nude photos.

6. **Vampire Limericks and Other Bits of Humor** – Limericks and cartoons.

7. **Sat the Selfish Bear** – A children's story.

8. **Exploring The Universe: The Art of Space** – A collection of photos of outer space as taken by the Hubble Space Telescope and other telescopes.

9. **My Life on eBay: or My Part-time Job for the Last 21 Years!** - A chronicle of my personal experiences, selling on eBay.

10. **"Black Men Skin Care Guide"** – Learn about skin care issues such as ingrown hairs, dark spots, hyperpigmentation, razor bumps, sun damage and vitiligo.

More Books by Other Authors

1. **"If I Had The Eyes of a Lion, I Would See…"** by Paul Frea - A children's picture book revealing animals a lion would see.

2. **"If I Had The Eyes of an Astronomer, I Would See…"** by Paul Frea – A children's picture book showing objects in space that an astronomer would see.

3. **"A Guide to the 59 Funniest Videos on Youtube"** by James Eridani – Discover laughter, food and recipes with this guide to funny cooking videos on Youtube.

Copyright Notices